TANZANIA TRAVEL GUIDE

Beyond Zanzibar's beaches: Uncharted adventures in Tanzania's hidden gems and Tanzanian Safari Unveiled.

Gale T. Norman

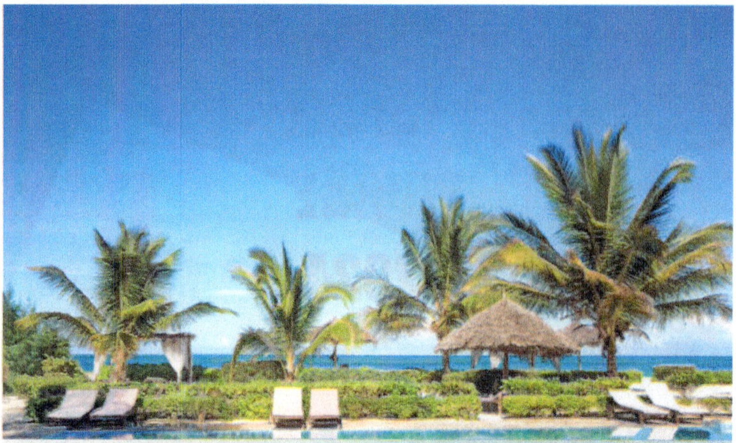
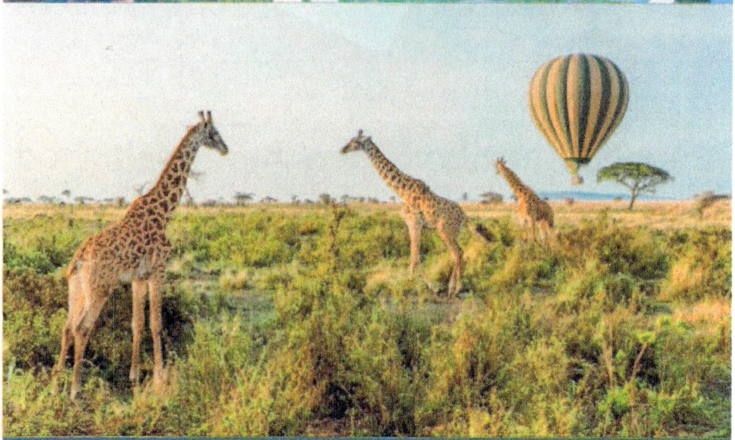
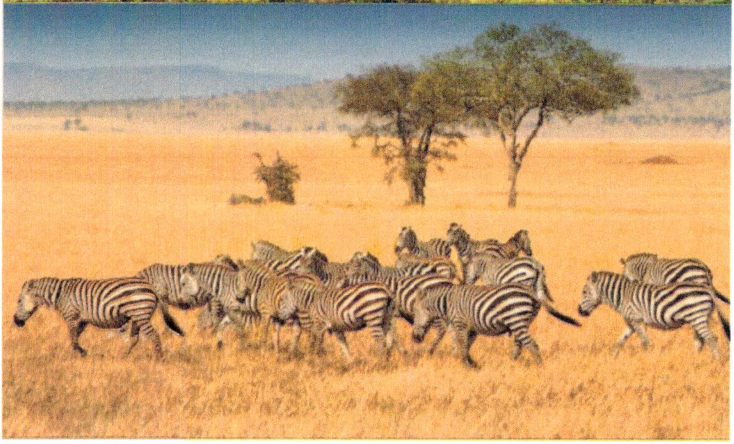

Khartoum
الخرطوم
Eritrea
صنعاء
Al Fashir
الفاشر
Nyala
نيالا
Djibouti
Dire Dawa
ድሬዳዋ
Ethiopia
South Sudan
Juba
Somalia
Mogadish
مقديشو
Uganda
Kisangani
Eldoret
Kenya
Kampala
Nairobi
Rwanda
cratic
blic of
ongo
Burundi
Arusha
Mombasa
Tanzania
Dar es Salaam
Comoros
Mayotte
Zambia
Malawi
Lusaka
Harare
Mozambique
Zimbabwe
An

Copyright Page

All rights reserved. No part of this publication may be reproduced, stored in a retrieval system, or transmitted in any form or by any means, electronic, mechanical, photocopying, recording, or otherwise, without prior written permission of Gale T Norman. The information contained in this publication is believed to be accurate and reliable; however, Gale T Norman does not assume any responsibility for any errors or omissions.

Copyright © 2024 Gale T Norman.

Table of Contents

Introduction — 7
    Brief overview of Tanzania — 8
    Geography and climate — 10
    Useful resources — 12

CHAPTER 1. Planning Your Trip — 15
    Best time to visit Tanzania — 15
    Entry requirements and visa information — 16
    Safety tips and travel insurance — 18
    Currency and payment options — 21

CHAPTER 2. Getting to Tanzania — 25
    International flights and major airports — 25
    Domestic transportation options — 28

CHAPTER 3. Top Tourist Destinations — 31
    Serengeti National Park — 31
    Wildlife and migration — 34
    Safari options and accommodations — 36
    Mount Kilimanjaro — 40
    Climbing routes and difficulty levels and, preparation and equipment needed — 42
    Zanzibar: Beaches and water activities — 45
    Historical sites and cultural experiences — 48
    Ngorongoro Conservation Area and Crater and wildlife — 52
    Cultural experiences with local tribes — 54

CHAPTER 4.Wildlife and Nature   57
   Tanzania's diverse ecosystems   57
   National parks, game reserves, unique wildlife species and bird watching spots   60

CHAPTER 5. Adventure and Outdoor Activities   65
   Hiking and trekking opportunities   65
   Tanzania, the jewel of East Africa, isn't just about spotting wildlife on thrilling safaris. It's a land begging to be explored on foot, where every step unveils a new vista, a hidden waterfall, or a glimpse into a world untouched by time. From scaling the continent's highest peak to weaving through misty rainforests, here's a taste of the incredible hiking and trekking opportunities Tanzania offers: 65
   Scuba diving and snorkeling in the Indian Ocean   68
   Canoeing and boating on Tanzania's lakes and rivers   71
   Hot air balloon safaris   74

CHAPTER 6. Cultural Experiences   78
   Unveiling the Soul of the Land: Encounters with Local Tribes   78
   Traditional music and dance   79
   Arts and crafts   79
   Visiting Local Markets and Villages   80

CHAPTER 7. Accommodation   83
   Luxurious Hotels and Resorts: 83
   Safari Lodges and Tented Camps: 83
   Guesthouses and Budget Options: 84
   CHAPTER 8. Dining and Cuisine   87
   Traditional Tanzanian dishes   87

Local Restaurants and Street Food	88
Dietary Considerations and Food Safety Tips	88
CHAPTER 9. Shopping and Souvenirs	**91**
Unique Tanzanian products and handicrafts	91
Best Places to Shop for Souvenirs	92
Bargaining Tips	92
CHAPTER 10 Health and Safety	**95**
Vaccination Requirements and Medical Facilities:	96
Malaria Prevention and Other Health Considerations:	96
Emergency Contacts and Local Laws:	97
CHAPTER 11. Language and Culture	**99**
Language	99
Cultural Etiquette	99
Cultural Sensitivity	100
Conclusion	**101**

Introduction

Dust billows behind the jeep, a tawny curtain chased by the wind across the Serengeti's endless plains. My heart thumps a wild counterpoint to the engine's purr, a drumbeat in my chest as we crest a rise. And then, there it is. Not a mirage, not a dream, but a living, breathing spectacle that sets the savannah ablaze.

The wildebeest migration. A million hooves pound the earth, a thunderous tattoo echoing across the golden expanse. Zebra stripes ripple like black and white brushstrokes against the emerald grass, and in the distance, a tawny pride of lions laze, nonchalant monarchs surveying their boundless kingdom.

It's more than a scene. It's a primal ballet, a raw symphony of survival played out on the world's grandest stage. The air hums with a tension both ancient and electric, the smell of sweat and dust and sheer life a primal perfume in my nostrils.

In that moment, time melts away. There's just the sun pounding down, the wind whipping my hair, and the breathtaking, heart-stopping panorama of nature playing out in front of me. I'm not a spectator, not a visitor, but a tiny thread woven into the fabric of this wild, magnificent tapestry.

As the sun dips below the horizon, painting the sky in fiery hues, the wildebeest surge on, a tide of life unstoppable and eternal. My jeep turns back, but the echo of that primal rhythm, the memory of a million hooves shaking the earth, remains etched in my soul. It's an experience that transcends words, a baptism by the raw beauty of Africa that leaves you forever changed.

This is Tanzania, not a photo in a brochure, but a pulse that beats beneath your skin, a memory that dances behind your eyelids long after you've left its sun-drenched shores. So pack your sense of wonder, your thirst for adventure, and come. Let Tanzania paint its story onto your soul, one unforgettable brushstroke at a time.

Brief overview of Tanzania

Tanzania: Where Lion Kings Roam and Spice Islands Bloom

Tanzania isn't a destination, it's a sensory explosion. Imagine sunrise over the Serengeti, painting the savannah with fiery streaks as a million wildebeest thunder across the plains. Feel the spray of the Indian Ocean on your face as you dive into coral reefs teeming with neon fish. Hike through misty rainforests where gorillas rustle the leaves and ancient baobab trees stand like sentinels. Breathe in the heady fragrance of cloves and cinnamon wafting from Zanzibar's spice markets. This is Tanzania, a land where adventure wears a thousand faces and every turn unveils a new story.

But Tanzania isn't just about wildlife and wilderness. Climb the snow-capped peak of Mount Kilimanjaro, Africa's highest roof, and feel the world shrink beneath your feet. Stroll through the cobbled streets of Stone Town, Zanzibar's ancient heart, where history whispers from crumbling coral houses and spice-laden scents hang heavy in the air. Soak up the vibrant rhythm of Dar es Salaam, a melting pot of cultures where modern skyscrapers rise above bustling markets overflowing with colorful fabrics and exotic fruits.

From the sun-drenched beaches of Mafia Island to the otherworldly Ngorongoro Crater, a volcanic jewel teeming with life, Tanzania's landscapes are as diverse as its people. Meet the Maasai in their ochre-painted robes, their fierce pride echoing in their chants and beaded jewelry. Learn about the Hadzabe tribe, the last true hunter-gatherers of East Africa, whose ancient traditions connect them to the land in a timeless dance.

Tanzania is a place where luxury whispers from tented camps hidden in the wilderness and budget escapes offer adventures under starlit skies. It's a land where time slows down, where the sun paints sunsets in fiery hues and the stars glitter like diamonds scattered across a velvet sky. It's a place that challenges you, surprises you, and leaves you forever changed.

So come, and explore the hidden corners of this East African gem. Let Tanzania weave its magic spell, one unforgettable experience at a time.

Geography and climate

A Land Shaped by Fire, Wind, and Water.

Tanzania isn't just a map; it's a story etched in mountains, sculpted by wind, and painted by rain. Imagine a canvas where volcanic scars meet shimmering lakes, where sun-baked plains surrender to emerald rainforests, and where the Indian Ocean laps at pristine shores. This is the geography of Tanzania, a land of breathtaking contrasts that shapes its climate and fuels its wild soul.

In the north, Mount Kilimanjaro, Africa's crown jewel, pierces the sky, its snow-capped summit a stark counterpoint to the sun-scorched savannahs below. This volcanic giant, born of fiery eruptions ages ago, is a testament to the power of nature's forge. Nearby, the Great Rift Valley, a geological gash splitting the land, cradles shimmering lakes like Tanganyika and Malawi, their depths whispering tales of ancient freshwater kingdoms.

Moving east, the landscape morphs into rolling plains, the Serengeti and Ngorongoro stretching like an emerald carpet punctuated by acacia trees. This vast grassland, where the annual wildebeest migration orchestrates a drama of survival, is a testament to the region's dry season winds that sculpt the land and whip the dust into towering clouds.

But Tanzania isn't all arid plains. In the northeast, lush mountains rise, cloaked in misty rainforests where ancient baobab trees guard secrets older than time. Here, the monsoons paint the landscape green, their rains feeding cascading waterfalls and nurturing a symphony of life beneath the emerald canopy.

Then, there's the magic of the Tanzanian coast. Picture palm-fringed beaches lapped by turquoise waters, a necklace of coral islands guarding the secrets of an underwater world. Zanzibar, an emerald jewel in the Indian Ocean, tempers the mainland's heat with balmy breezes and spicy scents, its history whispered in crumbling ruins and bustling markets.

This kaleidoscope of landscapes isn't just scenery; it shapes Tanzania's climate, creating a dance of seasons. The hot, dry months, when the savannah shimmers gold and the sun's grip is tight, give way to the drama of the rainy seasons, when skies unleash their fury and waterfalls roar back. Each season paints a different hue on this vibrant canvas, offering new adventures and landscapes to explore.

So, whether you seek the thrill of the Serengeti's endless plains, the cool embrace of mountain mists, or the sun-kissed bliss of tropical shores, Tanzania's diverse geography beckons. Come, discover this land where fire, wind, and water have conspired to create a tapestry of experiences as unique as they are unforgettable.

Useful resources

Mobile Apps:

- Maps.me: Download offline maps that work even without internet, saving you from getting lost in the bush.
- Wikitude: Augmented reality magic!Discover nearby points of interest,restaurants, and even wildlife through your phone's camera.
- Kiswahili Phrasebook: Brush up on basic Swahili greetings, essential phrases, and bargaining tactics – this app will have you conversing like a local in no time.

Don't Forget:

- Check current travel advisories and health recommendations from your government's travel advisory service.
- Invest in a good travel insurance that covers medical emergencies and trip cancellations.
- Pack a reusable water bottle and download offline e-books or podcasts for those in-between moments.

Embrace the spirit of adventure, pack your curiosity, and delve into this treasure trove of information. Remember, the best travel resource is your own open mind and sense of wonder – Tanzania awaits, ready to unveil its magic to you!

CHAPTER 1. Planning Your Trip

Best time to visit Tanzania

Deciding when to visit Tanzania is like picking the perfect spice for your safari stew – each season adds a unique flavor to your experience. So, buckle up for a taste of what each time of year brings:

Dry Days & Drama (June – October): This is peak season when the sun reigns supreme and the skies stay bone dry. It's like the Serengeti rolled out a red carpet for wildlife. The Great Migration thunders across the plains, rivers shrink to shimmering jewels, and predators come out to play on waterholes transformed into dramatic dinner theaters. Expect clear skies, perfect for Kilimanjaro climbs, and a lively buzz on the tourist trail. Just be prepared for higher prices and a touch of elbow-to-elbow exploring.

Green & Serene (November – March): The rains return, painting the landscapes emerald and turning roads into muddy ribbons. But don't pack your umbrella just yet! Sunshine still reigns, and the crowds thin out, leaving you with a more intimate safari experience. Expect lush landscapes, fewer jeeps vying for the best wildebeest shots, and bargain prices at lodges. Be warned, though, that some parks and roads close, and certain coastal areas experience heavier downpours.

Shoulder Season Serenity (April – May & May – June): These months bridge the gap between seasons, offering a sweet spot for budget-conscious adventurers. The rains taper off, leaving behind lush landscapes and fewer crowds. Prices dip, some roads reopen, and wildlife is still plentiful. Just be prepared for unpredictable weather, with scattered showers and the occasional muddy detour.

Beyond the Big Five: Of course, Tanzania isn't just about chasing wildebeest. For hikers, June to September boasts clear skies and steady temperatures on Kilimanjaro, while scuba divers will find the best underwater visibility in October and November. Zanzibar beckons with sunshine year-round, offering beach bliss regardless of the season.

So, no matter what your travel style or budget, Tanzania has a perfect season waiting for you. Just decide what kind of adventure you crave, pick your spice, and get ready to stir up an unforgettable Tanzanian experience.

Entry requirements and visa information

Tanzania, the crown jewel of East Africa, beckons with its majestic Serengeti, sapphire-blue coastal havens, and the ethereal summit of Kilimanjaro. But before you get swept away by the magic, let's navigate the practicalities. This guide will be your visa-to-vacation compass, untangling the entry requirements and ensuring a smooth landing in paradise.

1.Passport Power: Pack your trusty travel document, the key that unlocks Tanzania's treasures. Make sure it boasts at least six months of validity beyond your planned departure date, with a blank page ready to receive the visa stamp.

2.Visa Options: Your passport's country of origin determines your visa route. Some lucky folks, like citizens of the European Union and the United States, can waltz through immigration with a visa on arrival (VOA). Simply cough up $100 in cash (be prepared, card readers can be fickle) and voila, Tanzania is yours to explore for up to 90 days.

For others, the e-visa shines as your friendly portal. Head to the Tanzanian Immigration Services website (immigration.go.tz) and weave your application online. Fill in the forms, upload your passport photo, and pay the $50 fee – a small price for streamlined entry. Within a few days, the virtual gate swings open, and your e-visa grants you 30 days of Tanzanian adventures.

But what if your passport doesn't hold visa-on-arrival privileges, and the e-visa isn't an option? Fear not, intrepid traveler! Embark on the traditional route and visit your nearest Tanzanian embassy or consulate.

They'll guide you through the application process, which usually involves similar documents as the e-visa, plus additional requirements depending on your visa type.

3.Pro Tip: Whichever route you choose, remember: time is your friend. Apply for your visa well in advance to avoid last-minute scrambles.

4.Beyond the Visa: Immigration formalities aside, ensure you have proof of onward travel (a flight ticket out of Tanzania) and sufficient funds to cover your stay. Yellow fever vaccination is mandatory for everyone, and other vaccinations like hepatitis A and B are recommended. Finally, pack some US dollars, the currency of choice for tipping and smaller purchases.

With these entry essentials in your backpack, you're ready to embark on your Tanzanian odyssey. Remember, a little preparation goes a long way, ensuring a seamless transition from airport tarmac to the bustling streets of Zanzibar or the endless vistas of the Serengeti. So, breathe in the anticipation, grab your passport, and let's unlock the wonders of Tanzania, one visa stamp at a time!

Safety tips and travel insurance

Embarking on a Tanzanian adventure promises sights that sear into your memory, from the sun-drenched savannah teeming with wildlife to the turquoise waters lapping against Zanzibar's shores. But before you lose yourself in the magic, a bit of preparation can pave the way for a stress-free journey. Let's navigate the essential safety tips and travel insurance considerations to ensure your Tanzanian expedition hums along like a well-oiled safari jeep.

Safety First:

- Health is wealth: Get clued up on recommended vaccinations (think yellow fever, typhoid, and rabies) and pack a well-stocked first-aid kit. Malaria isn't a party crasher you want, so consult your doctor about anti-malarial medication. Mosquito nets are your nocturnal BFFs - befriend them.
- Be street smart: Petty theft lurks in crowded areas, so keep your valuables zipped up and close. Don't flash fancy cameras or phones, and leave the bling at home. Stick to well-lit streets after dark and avoid isolated areas, especially solo.
- Respect the locals: Dress modestly, especially in religious areas. Haggling is part of the fun at markets, but be respectful and avoid aggressive bargaining. Learn a few Swahili greetings - "Jambo" for hello goes a long way!

- Be wildlife-wise: Don't get too chummy with the wildebeest, no matter how tempting that selfie might be. Keep your distance from all animals, and stick with your guide in national parks. Remember, you're a visitor in their kingdom, so tread respectfully.

Insurance: Your Safety Net:

- Medical Emergencies: Let's face it, nobody plans for a broken bone on Kilimanjaro. Comprehensive travel insurance with robust medical coverage is your guardian angel, covering unexpected doctor visits, hospital stays, and even medical evacuation if needed.
- Trip Cancellations: Life throws curveballs, and sometimes your dream safari has to wait. Insurance with trip cancellation coverage can reimburse you for pre-paid expenses if illness, natural disasters, or other unforeseen events force you to scrap your plans.
- Baggage Blues: Lost luggage can turn your sunshine into grey skies. Travel insurance with baggage coverage can ease the sting, providing compensation for lost or damaged belongings.

Remember:

- Read the fine print: Before you click "buy" on that insurance policy, scrutinize the details. Understand exclusions, coverage limits, and any specific activities that might require additional riders.
- Shop around: Compare quotes from different providers to find the best fit for your needs and budget.
- Carry your policy: Don't leave your insurance tucked away in your email inbox. Print a copy and keep it in your travel documents, easily accessible in case of emergencies.

With a dash of caution and a smart insurance policy in your backpack, you can confidently embrace the wonders of Tanzania, knowing you're shielded from unexpected bumps in the road. So, pack your sense of adventure, lather on the sunscreen, and get ready to create memories that will outshine even the Serengeti sunrise. Hakuna Matata!

Currency and payment options

Navigating a new currency when traveling can feel like deciphering ancient hieroglyphics. Fear not, intrepid explorer! This guide will equip you with the knowledge to conquer Tanzanian shillings and navigate like a local pro.

The King of Cash:

The Tanzanian Shilling (TSH) reigns supreme. While US Dollars hold sway in tourist hotspots, for everyday purchases and local markets, embracing the shilling is key. Exchange some cash before arrival at reputable bureaus de change, and avoid tempting street exchanges like you'd dodge rogue hyenas. ATMs dispensing shillings are readily available in cities, but carry a backup card in case of technical gremlins.

Card Crusaders:

Credit cards are welcomed at swanky hotels and safari lodges, but expect a surcharge like a cheeky meerkat eyeing your picnic. Visa reigns supreme, while Mastercard might encounter some grumpy zebras (limited acceptance). For smaller shops and local vendors, plastic is rarely an option.

Mobile Money Magic:

Tanzania's tech scene is galloping ahead, and mobile money platforms like M-Pesa are transforming transactions. If you plan on staying longer, consider setting up a local SIM card and hopping on the mobile money bandwagon. It's a secure, convenient way to pay for everything from street food to souvenirs, leaving your bulky wallet safely tucked away.

Tipping Tales:

Tipping isn't mandatory, but a small gesture of appreciation for good service is always welcome. Round up a restaurant bill or offer a few thousand shillings to attentive guides or helpful locals. Remember, a little goes a long way, like a well-placed watering hole in the dry season.

Bonus Bits:

- Bargain with a smile! Haggling is expected at markets, but keep it fun and friendly, not a lion chasing its prey.
- Smaller denominations of shillings come in handy for tipping and small purchases.
- Don't flash your cash or valuables, keep them stashed safely away from prying eyes.
- Remember, you're a guest in Tanzania. Be respectful of local customs and traditions, and your journey will be enriched beyond measure.

So, ditch the decoder ring and embrace the Tanzanian way! With these tips and a healthy dose of common sense, your financial safari will be as smooth as a gazelle on the Serengeti plains. Hakuna Matata with your money matters!

CHAPTER 2. Getting to Tanzania

International flights and major airports

Tanzania, the land of soaring Mount Kilimanjaro and endless savannahs, beckons adventurous spirits from across the globe. But how do you navigate the gateway to this East African gem? Let's demystify the world of Tanzanian airports and international flights, ensuring your arrival is as smooth as a zebra gliding across the plains.

The Big Three:

- Julius Nyerere International Airport (DAR): This behemoth near Dar es Salaam is the main entry point, welcoming flights from around the world. Think of it as your launchpad for exploring the bustling coastal city, vibrant markets, and nearby Zanzibar Island.
- Kilimanjaro International Airport (JRO): Nestled near the majestic mountain, this airport caters to safari-seekers and adventurers yearning to climb Kili's rugged slopes. Prepare for breathtaking views and a touch of adrenaline upon arrival.
- Abeid Amani Karume International Airport (ZNZ): Zanzibar's crown jewel, this airport whisks you straight to turquoise waters, spice-scented alleys, and laid-back island vibes.

Picture pristine beaches and swaying palm trees just beyond the arrival gate.

Beyond the Big Three:

While the above trio handles most international arrivals, smaller airports like Mwanza in the north and Songo Songo in the south cater to regional flights and offer alternative entry points depending on your itinerary.

Flight Savvy Tips:

- Plan: Peak season brings a flurry of visitors, so book your flights early, especially if Kilimanjaro calls your name.
- Compare carriers: Airlines like Ethiopian Airlines, Qatar Airways, and Kenya Airways offer frequent connections, so shop around for the best deals and travel times.
- Consider stopovers: Nairobi in Kenya can be a convenient and affordable gateway, with onward connections to Tanzania.
- Visa check: Make sure your passport is valid and check visa requirements well in advance. The last thing you want is a bureaucratic bungle at the border.

Navigating Arrivals:

- Airport transfers: Pre-book a taxi or airport shuttle for a hassle-free ride to your destination, especially if arriving late at night.
- Local SIM cards: Stay connected by grabbing a local SIM card at the airport for affordable data and calls.
- Currency exchange: Don't be caught short! Exchange some cash into Tanzanian shillings at airport counters before venturing out.

Remember:

- Relax and enjoy the ride: Let the anticipation simmer as you soar toward Tanzania. The adventure begins the moment you touch down.
- Be patient: Customs and immigration queues can take time, so pack a book and embrace the Tanzanian pace of life.
- Ask for help: Don't hesitate to approach airport staff or fellow travelers if you need assistance. Everyone's here for the same reason – to experience the magic of Tanzania!

With this guide and a sprinkle of wanderlust, your arrival in Tanzania will be as effortless as a cheetah catching its lunch. So buckle up, adventurer, and prepare to touch down in paradise!

Domestic transportation options

Tanzania, with its sprawling savannas, vibrant cities, and dreamy Zanzibar Island, begs to be explored. But once you've touched down, how do you navigate the diverse landscapes and hidden corners? Fear not, wanderlust warriors! This guide will equip you with the know-how to conquer domestic transportation in Tanzania, ensuring your journey is as smooth as a gazelle on the Serengeti.

Road Warriors:

- Buses: The workhorses of Tanzanian travel, buses come in all flavors – luxurious coach liners with AC and Wi-Fi, rickety but charming dala-dalas (minibusses) bouncing through villages, and everything in between. Choose based on your budget and timeframe, but remember, scenic detours and unexpected delays are part of the charm!
- Trains: For a nostalgic adventure, hop on the Tanzania Railway Authority's network. The central line chugs past baobab trees and wildlife-rich reserves, while the coastal route hugs the Indian Ocean, offering salty breezes and dramatic scenery. Think affordable sleeper trains with a side of adventure.
- Taxis: Metered taxis are readily available in cities, but haggling is expected for unmetered

rides. For longer journeys, consider private car rentals with drivers, offering flexibility and comfort at a premium.

Airborne Escapades:

- Domestic flights: Need to jump across the country in a jiffy? Domestic airlines like Coastal Aviation and Auric Air connect major cities and remote safari airstrips with swift efficiency. Think of breathtaking aerial views and a fast track to your next adventure.

Island Hopping:

- Ferries: Zanzibar beckons with its turquoise waters and swaying palm trees. Ferries from Dar es Salaam and other coastal towns provide a budget-friendly option, with the journey itself a mini-adventure offering glimpses of local life and salty breezes. Think bobbing on the Indian Ocean with the promise of paradise on the horizon.

Bonus Tips:

- Dala-dalas: Embrace the local experience! These minibuses are a cultural immersion but be prepared for crowdedness and unpredictable schedules. Learn a few Swahili phrases and hang on for the ride!

- Hitchhiking: While common in rural areas, exercise caution and use your common sense. Stick to main roads and don't accept rides from strangers unless it feels completely safe.
- Download offline maps: GPS can be unreliable in remote areas, so pre-download offline maps and save yourself the navigation stress.

Remember:

- Time is relative: Tanzanian schedules operate on their rhythm. Patience and flexibility are your essential travel companions.
- Embrace the journey: The adventure isn't just about the destination. Soak in the sights, sounds, and encounters along the way – that's where the real magic lies.
- Ask for help: Locals are friendly and always willing to assist. Don't hesitate to ask for directions or recommendations, even if your Swahili is nonexistent.

With this guide in your backpack and a spirit of wanderlust, you're all set to conquer domestic travel in Tanzania. So hop on a bus, grab a window seat on a plane, or hitch a ride with a friendly local – the roads of Tanzania await, bursting with adventure and unforgettable experiences. Hakuna Matata on your travels!

CHAPTER 3. Top Tourist Destinations

Serengeti National Park

The Jewel of Tanzania:

Serengeti, a UNESCO World Heritage Site, isn't just a park; it's an ecosystem pulsating with life. Over 1.5 million wildebeests and 250,000 zebras embark on the world's greatest animal migration each year, a breathtaking spectacle that draws adventurers from across the globe. But the Serengeti's magic extends far beyond the hooves.

Beyond the Migration:

- Predator Prowess: Witness the grace of cheetahs sprinting across the plains, the stealth of leopards stalking in the shadows, and the power of crocodiles lurking in watering holes. Serengeti houses the largest lion population in Africa, their golden manes glinting against the midday sun.
- Birdwatcher's Paradise: Over 500 bird species soar through the skies, from elegant ostriches strutting across the plains to vibrant flocks of pink flamingos painting the soda lakes with color. Keep your eyes peeled for eagles, owls, and the

elusive secretarybird, stalking the grasslands with its prehistoric grace.
- Diverse Landscapes: The Serengeti's beauty isn't limited to endless plains. Explore kopjes, and rocky outcrops that offer panoramic views and shelter elusive rock hyraxes. Venture into acacia woodlands, where elephants trumpet greetings and giraffes nibble on the highest leaves.

Planning Your Safari:

- When to Go: The Great Migration is the crown jewel, with herds crossing the Mara River between July and October. However, the Serengeti offers magic year-round. The dry season (June to October) brings clear skies and abundant wildlife around waterholes. The wet season (November to May) paints the landscape green and attracts newborn animals.
- Where to Stay: Choose from luxurious lodges with infinity pools overlooking the plains to cozy tented camps offering immersive experiences. Budget-friendly campsites are also available for adventurous travelers.
- How to Explore: Game drives in open jeeps are the classic way to experience the Serengeti. Hot air balloon safaris offer stunning aerial views while walking safaris provide an intimate encounter with the landscape.

Beyond the Jeep:

- Meet the Maasai: Immerse yourself in the rich culture of the Maasai people, visiting their villages and learning about their traditions.
- Stargazing Extravaganza: With minimal light pollution, the Serengeti's night sky explodes with a million stars. Witness constellations dance across the darkness, feeling a profound connection to the vastness of the universe.

Remember:

- Respect the wildlife: Maintain a safe distance, avoid loud noises, and never litter. This is their home, and we are mere guests.
- Dress for the occasion: Comfortable clothes, sturdy shoes, a hat, and sunscreen are essential. Binoculars and a camera will help you capture those unforgettable moments.
- Leave no trace: Pack out all your trash and respect the park's fragile ecosystem.

The Serengeti awaits, a canvas painted with the raw beauty of nature. Come witness the dance of life, the rhythm of the wild, and the greatest show on Earth. Let the wind ruffle your hair, the dust settles on your skin, and the memories of this awe-inspiring land etch themselves forever in your soul.

Hakuna Matata on your Tanzanian adventure!

Wildlife and migration

Tanzania, the cradle of humanity, pulsates with a rhythm all its own. Here, on vast savannas and in acacia-dotted woodlands, unfolds a drama wilder than any Hollywood script. It's a stage where millions of hooves thunder, predators stalk with silent grace, and nature paints its canvas with vibrant hues of life.

The Greatest Show on Earth: No story of Tanzania's wildlife can begin without the Serengeti National Park, where the world's greatest animal migration takes center stage. Imagine 1.5 million wildebeests and 250,000 zebras thundering across the plains, a tide of hooves driven by an ancient instinct. Witnessing this spectacle, as they cross crocodile-infested rivers and navigate perilous landscapes, is to feel the raw power of nature coursing through your veins.

Beyond the Big Show: Tanzania's wildlife tapestry is woven with threads far richer than just wildebeests. In the Serengeti itself, cheetahs blur across the plains in a blur of spots, leopards prowl the shadows with stealthy elegance, and lions rule their kingdoms with regal nonchalance. Elephants trumpet their greetings, giraffes stretch their necks to impossible heights, and over 500 bird species paint the sky with vibrant wings.

Venturing Beyond the Serengeti: Tanzania's wildlife mosaic extends far beyond the Serengeti's borders. In the Ngorongoro Crater, a collapsed volcano cradles a unique ecosystem where black rhinos graze, black-and-white colobus monkeys swing through the trees, and giant African eagles survey the scene from above.

Tarangire National Park boasts the highest elephant density in Africa, while the Selous Game Reserve shelters elusive wild dogs and the largest population of black rhinoceroses in East Africa. In Lake Manyara National Park, tree-climbing lions lounge lazily in acacia branches, while hippos wallow in the cool waters below.

Remembering the Rhythm: Each park, each ecosystem, beats to its drum. The Great Migration might be the headliner, but Tanzania's wildlife symphony has countless captivating movements. It's in the silent stalk of a hunting cheetah, the playful squabble of meerkats, and the flash of iridescent feathers as a hummingbird sips nectar.

Tips for Your Wildlife Encounter:

Respect the Wild: This is their kingdom, and we are mere guests. Maintain a safe distance, avoid loud noises, and never litter. Remember, responsible tourism benefits both wildlife and communities.

Dress for Adventure: Comfortable clothes, sturdy shoes, a hat, and sunscreen are essential. Consider binoculars and a camera with a good zoom to capture those once-in-a-lifetime moments.

Choose the Right Time: The dry season (June to October) offers clear skies and concentrated wildlife around waterholes, while the wet season (November to May) paints the landscape green and attracts newborn animals.

Embrace the Unexpected: Nature doesn't follow a script. Be prepared for the unexpected, for an elusive leopard sighting or a dramatic thunderstorm that transforms the plains into a shimmering lake.

Tanzania's wildlife is a gift, a story etched in fur, feathers, and hoofprints. Come, witness the dance of life, the pulse of Africa, and let the memories of this awe-inspiring land echo forever in your soul. Hakuna Matata!

Safari options and accommodations

Tanzania's vast savannas and dramatic landscapes beckon adventurous souls with promises of wildlife encounters that leave you breathless. But choosing the right safari experience can feel like navigating a maze of jeeps, tents, and price tags. Fear not, intrepid explorer! This guide will unravel the mysteries of Tanzanian safaris, ensuring you find the perfect match for your budget and travel style.

Budget Beacons:

Camping: Embrace the raw spirit of the bush with a camping safari. Pitch your tent or opt for pre-set options, huddle around crackling campfires under starry skies, and share stories with fellow adventurers. Budget-friendly, yes, but remember, comfort comes with its price tag (or lack thereof).

Community-Run Camps: Immerse yourself in local culture and support conservation efforts by choosing a community-run camp. These often offer basic but comfortable accommodations, delicious local cuisine, and a chance to directly connect with the people who call Tanzania home.

Mid-Range Marvels:

Mobile Tented Camps: Crave comfort without sacrificing flexibility? Mobile tented camps move with the seasons and the wildlife, setting up camp in prime viewing locations. Imagine waking up to the trumpeting of elephants just beyond your canvas walls – an experience etched in memory forever.

Permanent Tented Camps: Offering a touch more permanence than their mobile counterparts, these camps provide comfortable tents with en-suite bathrooms and stunning views. You'll still feel connected to the wilderness, but with a hot shower and a comfy bed at the end of the day.

Luxury Lodges:

Boutique Lodges: For an intimate and personalized experience, boutique lodges offer smaller guest numbers, exceptional service, and often unique architectural blends with the surrounding landscape. Think plunge pools overlooking watering holes, gourmet meals served under starry skies, and attentive guides leading you to unforgettable wildlife encounters.

Classic Safari Lodges: Immerse yourself in the golden age of African safaris with a stay at a classic lodge. These often boast colonial-style architecture, spacious rooms with verandas, and communal areas designed for sharing stories and laughter over sundowners. Expect impeccable service, gourmet dining, and a touch of timeless elegance.

Beyond the Bed:

Remember, your safari experience extends beyond the walls of your tent or lodge. Think about these things before selecting:

Location: Will you be in the heart of the Serengeti, exploring the Ngorongoro Crater, or venturing off the beaten path? Choose a base camp that puts you closest to the action you crave.

Activities: Do you dream of balloon safaris soaring over the plains, walking safaris following in the footsteps of elephants, or game drives led by expert guides? Ensure your chosen accommodation offers the activities that make your pulse quicken.

Sustainability: Responsible tourism matters. Choose operators committed to conservation efforts and supporting local communities.

Safari Savvy Tips:

Book Early: Peak season sees lodges fill up fast, so plan your trip well in advance, especially during the Great Migration.

Pack Wisely: Comfortable clothes, sturdy shoes, binoculars, and a good camera are essentials. Remember, layers are key for unpredictable weather changes.

Embrace the Unexpected: Wildlife sightings are never guaranteed, but that's part of the magic. Be flexible, keep your eyes peeled, and savor every moment, even the quiet ones.

Tanzania's safaris are not just vacations; they're transformative experiences that etch themselves onto your soul. So, choose your adventure wisely, pack your sense of wonder, and prepare to be swept away by the magic of the Tanzanian wilderness. Hakuna Matata, and enjoy the ride!

Mount Kilimanjaro

Towering above the Tanzanian plains, Mount Kilimanjaro isn't just a mountain; it's a behemoth, a titan, a whispered legend made real. Its snow-capped peak pierces the sky, beckoning adventurers from across the globe to test their grit against its formidable slopes.

Three Faces, One Dream: Kilimanjaro isn't one mountain, but three volcanic cones: Kibo, the summit, Mawenzi, the second-highest, and Shira, the elder giant. Climbing Kilimanjaro means traversing a landscape that shifts from lush rainforest to barren moonscapes, a journey through microclimates as diverse as the dreams it inspires.

A Trek for Every Soul: Don't be fooled by Kilimanjaro's lofty summit – it's a climb for every level of trekker. Choose from five established routes, each offering its challenges and rewards. The Marangu Route, dubbed the "Coca-Cola Route," offers well-maintained paths and basic huts, while the Machame Route rewards with stunning scenery and diverse ecosystems. For seasoned climbers, the Barranco Wall on the Rongai Route promises a thrilling scramble, and the challenging Umbwe Valley trek tests even the most experienced legs.

Beyond the Ascent: Scaling Kilimanjaro isn't just about ticking a box; it's a transformative experience. You'll sweat alongside strangers who become allies, sharing moments of shared exhaustion and breathtaking vistas. You'll push your limits, discover hidden reserves of strength, and emerge from the clouds a different person, forever marked by the magic of Africa's roof.

Remember:

- Prepare Early: Kilimanjaro demands respect. Choose your route, train diligently, and acclimatize to the altitude. It's not just a climb; it's a commitment.
- Respect the Mountain: Leave no trace, follow conservation guidelines, and remember, you're a guest in this breathtaking ecosystem.

- Embrace the Journey: Every step, every stumble, and every sunrise over the clouds is part of the Kilimanjaro experience. Savor it all, because reaching the summit is just the beginning of the memories you'll carry forever.

So, pack your sense of adventure, lace up your boots, and set your sights on Kilimanjaro. Africa's crown jewel awaits, ready to etch its legend onto your soul. Hakuna Matata, and climb well!

Climbing routes and difficulty levels and, preparation and equipment needed

Mount Kilimanjaro isn't a quick jaunt to the park; it's a bona fide expedition demanding respect and preparation. Before setting your sights on the summit, here's the lowdown on crucial rules, challenging realities, and essential gear you'll need to tame this African giant.

Rules & Respect:

Park Permits: Acquire the necessary climbing permits well in advance. Every step on Kilimanjaro falls within a protected national park, and supporting conservation efforts starts with proper paperwork.

Leave No Trace: Pack out all your trash. Kilimanjaro's beauty shouldn't be tarnished by discarded wrappers or careless footprints. Embrace sustainable practices and respect the mountain's fragile ecosystem.

Stay on the Path: Designated trails weave through diverse landscapes, protecting both trekkers and the delicate mountain environment. Sticking to the path ensures a safer climb for everyone.

Facing the Challenge:

This isn't a walk-in park. Avoid attitude sickness Kilimanjaro sits at 19,341 feet, and altitude sickness (AMS) can be a serious threat. Choose a gradual ascent route, listen to your body, and acclimatize properly to avoid potentially life-threatening symptoms.

Weather Whims: From scorching sunshine to snowstorms, Kilimanjaro's weather throws curveballs. Be prepared for anything with layered clothing, sturdy footwear, and a flexible mindset. Remember, patience is your ultimate weapon against unpredictable skies.

Physical Rigor: This isn't a stroll through the mall. You'll trek for days, carrying your gear, battling elevation, and pushing your physical limits. Train beforehand, build endurance, and listen to your body's whispers of fatigue.

Gearing Up for Glory:

Durable Boots: Your feet will thank you for investing in high-quality hiking boots with good traction. Think waterproof, ankle-support, and comfortable on rugged terrain.

Layering is Key: Pack clothes for all weather conditions – warm base layers, insulating mid-layers, and a waterproof outer shell. Remember, the temperature drops dramatically as you climb.

Hydration Hero: Pack a sturdy water bottle or hydration pack and stay hydrated throughout the trek. Altitude dehydrates faster, so keep that H2O flowing.

Headlamp Essential: Darkness falls quickly on the mountain. A reliable headlamp with extra batteries is crucial for navigating nighttime bathroom breaks and early morning starts.

Bonus Tips:

Hire a reputable guide with local knowledge and experience navigating Kilimanjaro's challenges.

Pack essentials like sunscreen, sunglasses, a first-aid kit, and medication for altitude sickness.

Embrace the journey! The climb is as much about the mental and emotional test as it is about reaching the summit. Savor the scenery, the camaraderie, and the awe-inspiring beauty of Africa's highest peak.

Remember, Kilimanjaro isn't a competition; it's a personal triumph. With proper preparation, respect for the mountain, and the right gear, you can conquer the Roof of Africa and etch an unforgettable journey onto your soul. Hakuna Matata, and climb strong!

Zanzibar: Beaches and water activities

Zanzibar, Tanzania's jewel in the Indian Ocean, isn't just a beach haven; it's a sensory feast. Picture soft, powdery sand whispering beneath your toes, turquoise waters shimmering like spilled jewels, and spice-scented breezes dancing through swaying palms. Zanzibar beckons with its sun-kissed shores, but its aquatic playground offers adventures far beyond the beach towel.

Beach Bliss:

- Nungwi: Zanzibar's crown jewel, Nungwi boasts a picture-perfect beach with powdery sand, calm waters, and vibrant coral reefs just offshore. Imagine lazy days under swaying palm umbrellas and evenings lit by bonfires with the rhythm of the waves as your soundtrack.

- Kendwa: Crave vibrant energy? Kendwa's your jam. This lively beach buzzes with watersports, bustling beach bars, and a party-under-the-stars vibe. Learn to kitesurf, kayak through mangrove forests, or simply sip cocktails as the sun dips into the horizon.
- Matemwe: Seek serenity? Matemwe whispers peace. This secluded stretch of coast offers unspoiled beauty, gentle waves, and a laid-back atmosphere. Picture serene beachfront lodges, yoga retreats under swaying palms, and days spent snorkeling in coral gardens teeming with colorful life.

Watersports Wonderland:

- Dive into Paradise: Zanzibar's coral reefs are underwater kingdoms bursting with vibrant colors and curious creatures. Scuba dive with majestic manta rays and playful turtles or snorkel alongside clownfish and shimmering angelfish.
- Catch the Perfect Wave: Surfers rejoice! Zanzibar's east coast boasts powerful swells that will test your skills and thrill your soul. Whether you're a seasoned shredder or a curious beginner, lessons are available to help you carve your way through the waves.
- Get Your Wind Up: Kitesurfing becomes addictive against the backdrop of Zanzibar's

turquoise waters. Harness the wind, feel the adrenaline surge as you skim the surface, and experience the island from a breathtaking bird's-eye view.

Beyond the Beach:

- Spice Up Your Life: Immerse yourself in Zanzibar's rich history and fragrant past. Explore bustling Stone Town, a UNESCO World Heritage Site, and wander through narrow alleyways lined with spice-laden shops. Learn about the island's role in the spice trade and pick up fragrant souvenirs to tantalize your taste buds back home.
- Dolphin Dance: Embark on a magical dolphin-watching tour. Witness these playful creatures frolicking in the waves, leaping and spinning in dazzling displays of joy. Capture their vibrant energy and feel a deep connection to the wonders of the natural world.
- Sunset Dhow Cruise: Bid farewell to the day with a romantic dhow cruise. Sail gracefully across the Indian Ocean as the sun paints the sky in fiery hues. Unwind with local music, delicious seafood, and the whisper of the wind in your hair.

Remember:

- Respect the local culture. Dress modestly when away from the beach and be mindful of local customs.
- Support sustainable tourism. Choose responsible operators who give back to the community and protect the island's fragile ecosystem.
- Embrace the island pace. Zanzibar isn't about rushing; it's about savoring the moments, the sunsets, and the smiles.

Zanzibar is more than just a beach paradise; it's a kaleidoscope of experiences waiting to be discovered. So, dive into its emerald waters, explore its spice-scented alleys, and let the rhythm of the island weave its magic into your soul. Hakuna Matata, and explore Zanzibar to your heart's content!

Historical sites and cultural experiences

Zanzibar, Tanzania's spice-scented isle, isn't just a beachcomber's haven. Its coral shores whisper tales of ancient sultans, daring dhows, and a vibrant cultural tapestry woven over centuries. So, dust off your explorer's hat and dive into Zanzibar's rich history and the captivating customs that still pulse through its narrow streets.

Stone Town: Echoes of Empires:

Wander Through Time: Stone Town, a UNESCO World Heritage Site, is Zanzibar's beating heart. Lose yourself in its labyrinthine alleys, where intricately carved wooden doors whisper stories of Omani sultans and Portuguese explorers. Marvel at the coral-stone architecture, a fusion of Arab, Indian, and European influences that tells the island's complex past.

Palace Secrets: Peek behind the grand doors of the opulent Beit al-Sahel, the sultan's former palace. Explore its ornate courtyards, admire the intricately painted ceilings, and imagine the whispers of power that once echoed through these walls.

Slave Trade Scars: Confront the island's darker history at the House of Wonders, a former slave market turned museum. Learn about Zanzibar's role in the brutal slave trade, a sobering reminder of the island's past, and pay respect to those who suffered beneath its shadow.

Cultural Tapestry of Zanzibar:

Drums in the Twilight: Savor the island's vibrant music scene. Catch a taarab performance, a captivating blend of Arab and African influences, where hypnotic rhythms and soulful vocals paint stories in the air. Or, lose yourself in the infectious beat of Ngoma drums, a traditional dance that celebrates Zanzibar's rich heritage.

Spice Sensations: Zanzibar's soul lies in its spices. Embark on a sensory journey through bustling spice markets, letting the pungent scents of cloves, nutmeg, and cinnamon fill your senses. Learn about their culinary and medicinal uses, and pick up fragrant souvenirs to taste Zanzibar's home.

Henna's Hidden Language: Explore the delicate art of henna. Watch as skilled henna artists transform hands and feet into intricate canvases, each swirling design conveying hidden meanings and messages passed down through generations.

Beyond Stone Town:

Jozani Forest Escapade: Venture into the enchanting Jozani Forest, a refuge for red colobus monkeys, playful butterflies, and ancient baobab trees. Trek through mangrove forests, spot endemic birds flitting through the canopy, and witness the island's rich biodiversity up close.

Dhow Dreams: Set sail on a traditional dhow, a wooden sailboat that has graced Zanzibar's waters for centuries. Feel the wind in your hair and the sun on your skin as you cruise along the turquoise coastline, experiencing the island's rhythm from a bygone era.

Village Rhythms: Step outside the tourist bubble and explore Zanzibar's charming villages. Mingle with locals at bustling markets, bargain for handcrafted souvenirs, and experience the warm hospitality that defines the island spirit.

Remember:

Respect local customs. Consider local sensitivities and dress modestly when visiting places of worship.

Learn a few Swahili phrases. A simple "Jambo" (hello) goes a long way in welcoming smiles and sparking meaningful connections.

Embrace the Zanzibar pace. Slow down, savor the moments, and let the island's enchanting rhythm weave its magic into your soul.

Zanzibar is more than just a beach paradise; it's a cultural mosaic waiting to be explored. So, wander through ancient alleys, feel the pulse of vibrant music, and taste the island's rich history in every spice-infused bite. Hakuna Matata, and discover the soul of Zanzibar!

Ngorongoro Conservation Area and Crater and wildlife

Tanzania's Ngorongoro Crater isn't just a hole in the ground; it's an Eden carved by fire and teeming with life. Imagine a colossal volcanic caldera cradling a vibrant ecosystem, where lions stalk under acacia trees, wildebeests thunder across the plains, and a cast of creatures big and small put on a daily show for awestruck travelers. But Ngorongoro is more than just a wildlife spectacle; it's a conservation success story whispering lessons of harmony between humans and nature.

Crater Carnivores: Descend into the crater's depths and become a silent observer in this natural amphitheater. Watch as majestic lions survey their kingdom from rocky outcrops, cheetahs blur across the plains in a flash of spots, and hyenas cackle over scavenged scraps. Don't forget to look up – graceful eagles soar on thermals, while vultures circle on patient wings, reminding you of the circle of life in all its raw beauty.

Beyond the Big Cats: Ngorongoro's stage isn't reserved for just the apex predators. Zebra stripes ripple across the grasslands like liquid dreams, playful meerkats stand sentinel on sun-baked rocks, and hundreds of bird species paint the sky with vibrant wings. Keep your eyes peeled for elusive black rhinos and the graceful silhouettes of giraffes reaching for the highest leaves.

Conservation with Conviction: The Ngorongoro Conservation Area isn't just a wildlife haven; it's a model for sustainable co-existence. Here, the Maasai people continue their centuries-old traditions of grazing livestock alongside wild animals, proving that humans and nature can thrive together. Their presence adds a unique cultural layer to the Ngorongoro experience, offering glimpses into a timeless way of life.

Beyond the Crater Rim: Don't let the crater walls confine your adventure. Explore the vast Ngorongoro Conservation Area itself, where rolling grasslands meet acacia woodlands and ancient volcanic peaks pierce the sky. Hike through the Ol Doinyo Lengai volcano, trek among elephants in the Empakaai Crater, or visit the Olduvai Gorge, a cradle of humanity where prehistoric secrets lie buried.

Ngorongoro Nuggets:

- Respect the Wildlife: Maintain a safe distance, refrain from loud noises, and leave no trace. This is their home, and we are mere guests.
- Dress for Adventure: Comfortable clothes, sturdy shoes, a hat, and sunscreen are essential. Binoculars and a camera with a good zoom will

help you capture those once-in-a-lifetime moments.
- Choose the Right Time: The dry season (June to October) offers clearer skies and concentrated wildlife around waterholes, while the wet season (November to May) paints the landscape green and attracts newborn animals.

Ngorongoro Crater isn't just a bucket list tick; it's an experience that etches itself onto your soul. So, stand on the crater rim, feel the wind whisper stories of ancient eruptions, and witness the ballet of life unfolding below. It's a reminder that even in the harshest landscapes, nature's resilience and beauty persevere. Hakuna Matata, and let Ngorongoro magic your heart away!

Cultural experiences with local tribes

Ngorongoro Crater isn't just a wildlife spectacle; it's a human story etched in ancient hills and echoing through the voices of the Maasai people. Immerse yourself in their vibrant culture, a timeless tapestry woven with age-old traditions, warm smiles, and a deep connection to the land.

Sharing a Boma: Step into a Maasai "boma," a circular enclosure of mud huts huddled together under the vast African sky. Witness their daily rhythm – women beading intricate jewelry, warriors adorned with ochre and feathers, and children chasing goats across the dusty plains. Share a meal of grilled meat and ugali (cornmeal porridge), savoring the flavors and soaking in the shared laughter.

Legends in Leather: Listen as elders weave tales of creation, tales whispered across generations and carried on the wind. Learn about their reverence for the lion, their spiritual connection to the land, and the fierce pride that defines their warrior traditions. Watch as young men leap high in the "adumu" jumping dance, testing their skills and proving their bravery.

Handover of Beads: Immerse yourself in the intricate world of Maasai beadwork. Each vibrant color and intricate pattern carries meaning – family lineage, personal triumphs, and even warnings. Learn the art of crafting your bracelet or necklace, carrying a piece of Maasai culture back home as a precious memory.

Beyond the Boma: Venture into the vast Ngorongoro plains alongside Maasai herders. Walk in their footsteps, learn the secrets of tracking wildlife, and understand their intricate relationship with the animals they share the land with. Witness the "moran," young warriors, tending their cattle, their spears a symbol of both protection and responsibility.

Remember:

Respect their Traditions: Dress modestly, ask permission before taking photos, and be mindful of cultural sensitivities. A simple greeting in broken Swahili goes a long way in fostering connection.

Support their Crafts: Purchase handcrafted souvenirs directly from Maasai artisans, ensuring fair trade and supporting their livelihoods.

Leave No Trace: Pack out any trash and minimize your environmental impact.

Recall that you are a visitor to their country.

Ngorongoro's magic extends beyond the crater rim. By interacting with the Maasai people, you unlock a deeper understanding of this land, its history, and its vibrant soul. So, open your heart to their warmth, listen to their stories, and feel the beat of a culture as timeless as the Ngorongoro itself. Hakuna Matata, and embrace the spirit of the Maasai!

CHAPTER 4. Wildlife and Nature

Tanzania's diverse ecosystems

Exploring Tanzania's Wildly Diverse Ecosystems

Tanzania isn't just a country; it's a continent compressed into one vibrant, dynamic nation. From snow-capped peaks piercing the heavens to sun-drenched shores lapped by the Indian Ocean, its landscapes shift and morph like a chameleon on caffeine. This dizzying diversity extends far beyond the eye-catching scenery, though. Tanzania's true magic lies in the kaleidoscope of ecosystems that paint its land, each teeming with unique life and bursting with untamed energy.

1. Where Mountains Cradle Clouds: The Eastern Arc Mountains

Imagine emerald jewels scattered across a sunbaked savanna. That's the Eastern Arc, a string of ancient mountains draped in misty forests that have defied the erosive grip of time. Here, monkeys swing through ancient trees bearded with Spanish moss, and shy bongos, the antelope of the shadows, tread through cathedral-like glades dappled with sunlight. Hike to the rim of a hidden crater lake, its surface reflecting the sky like a shattered mirror, or lose yourself in the symphony of birdsong that fills the cool, fern-carpeted air.

2. Where Land Meets Water: The Serengeti and Beyond

The Serengeti isn't just a national park; it's a primal heartbeat that drums across the vast savannas of Tanzania. Here, where golden grasslands stretch to the horizon and acacia trees claw at the endless sky, nature stages the greatest wildlife show on Earth. Witness the annual migration, a million hooves thundering across the plains as wildebeest and zebra flee parched lands in search of life-giving rain. Watch a pride of lions basking in the golden dawn, their tawny coats shimmering like molten gold, or spot solitary leopards draped across branches like living jewels.

But the Serengeti is just the first act. Venture further and discover the otherworldly beauty of the Ngorongoro Crater, a collapsed volcano teeming with wildlife, or lose yourself in the endless plains of Tarangire National Park, where elephant herds wander like gray giants amidst baobab trees that whisper secrets of the ages.

3. Where the Ocean Breathes: The Tanzanian Coast

Swap your safari boots for flip-flops as you trade the ochre savannas for the turquoise embrace of the Indian Ocean. Tanzania's coastline is a string of pearls, each island whispering its siren song. Zanzibar, with its spice-scented alleys and beaches fringed with swaying palms, beckons with the promise of lazy days and balmy nights. Mafia Island, a verdant jewel fringed by coral reefs teeming with Technicolor fish, invites divers to explore an underwater kaleidoscope. And Pemba, with its hidden coves and lush forests, offers a taste of island life untouched by time.

But the magic extends beyond the beaches. Glide through mangrove forests where monkeys chatter from the emerald canopy or kayak past flamingo-painted lagoons where the water shimmers like liquid silver. Snorkel alongside gentle giants in the turquoise haven of Mnemba Atoll, or cast your line into the endless blue, the thrill of the catch rivaled only by the breathtaking beauty of the horizon.

4. Where Fire and Water Collide: The Great Rift Valley

The Great Rift Valley isn't just a scar across the earth; it's a crucible where nature forges some of its most awe-inspiring landscapes. Here, volcanic craters smolder like angry eyes, their slopes cloaked in mist and mystery. Lake Natron, a flamingo-painted jewel nestled in the shadow of an active volcano, stuns with its flamingo-flocked shores and caustic waters that turn birds to stone. Deep within the Ngorongoro Conservation Area, the Empakaai Crater, a verdant oasis ringed by volcanic cliffs, hides a secret lake that whispers tales of ancient civilizations.

5. Where Time Stands Still: The Southern Highlands

Tanzania's heart beats not just in the savannas and on the coast, but also in the emerald embrace of the Southern Highlands. Here, rolling hills draped in tea plantations stretch towards the horizon, and ancient towns whisper stories of colonial settlers and forgotten empires. Hike through the Udzungwa Mountains, a lush tapestry woven with waterfalls and hidden valleys, or climb the vertiginous slopes of Mount Kito, its peak piercing the clouds like a celestial spear. And as the sun dips below the horizon, casting long shadows across the verdant hills, find solace in the timeless beauty of a land where time itself seems to slow.

Tanzania is a land where ecosystems collide and landscapes morph, a living tapestry woven from fire and water, mountain and sea. So lace up your boots, grab your snorkel, and prepare to be dazzled.

National parks, game reserves, unique wildlife species and bird watching spots

Forget cookie-cutter safaris - Tanzania unveils a vibrant mosaic of national parks and game reserves, each brimming with unique wildlife and dazzling watery havens. From colossal beasts thundering across sun-baked plains to elusive primates swinging through ancient forests, here's a dip into Tanzania's wild wonders:

1. Serengeti and Ngorongoro: Where Legends Run Wild

The Serengeti isn't just a park; it's a primal heartbeat echoing across endless grasslands. Witness the annual migration, a million hooves drumming the earth as wildebeests and zebras chase life-giving rains. Watch lions, their manes aflame in the dawn, stalk prey amongst golden grasses. Then, descend into the Ngorongoro Crater, a volcanic Eden teeming with elephants, rhinos, and even the rare black rhino – a mythical gem amidst the wilderness.

2. Beyond the Big Five: Unmasking Hidden Treasures

While the Serengeti basks in its fame, Tanzania's wild holds secrets waiting to be unraveled. In Tarangire, baobab trees, like timeworn sentinels, watch over elephant herds lumbering through dry-season landscapes. Ruaha, the forgotten giant, sprawls southward, whispering tales of elusive leopards, buffalo herds, and the endangered wild dog. And for true off-the-beaten-path adventures, Katavi beckons with crocodiles basking along the mighty Rukwa River, a prehistoric tableau come to life.

3. Where Mountains Embrace Water: Lake Manyara and the Eastern Arc

Not all Tanzanian magic unfolds on flat plains. Nestled in the Rift Valley's shadow, Lake Manyara unveils a serene jewel where hippos wallow in shallows, monkeys chatter from lush forests, and tree-climbing lions survey their domain from lofty branches. Venture east, and the mist-shrouded peaks of the Eastern Arc beckon. Hike rainforests dripping with orchids and ferns, spot shy bongos flitting through the undergrowth, and discover hidden waterfalls cascading into emerald pools – a symphony of nature in its purest form.

4. Ocean Meets Wilderness: Saadani and Mikumi

Trade dust for sea spray in Saadani National Park, where golden beaches hug mangrove forests and elephants stroll along the shore. Watch dolphins frolic in turquoise waves, and kayak through mangrove channels teeming with exotic birdlife. In Mikumi, lions roar their nightly chorus beneath a star-studded sky, while zebras graze on sun-drenched plains and giraffes tower over acacia trees. This park, near Dar es Salaam, makes a perfect day trip or add-on to your Tanzanian adventure.

5. A Climber's Dream: Scaling Kilimanjaro and Beyond

For those seeking a challenge that goes beyond wildlife spotting, Mount Kilimanjaro beckons. This snow-capped behemoth, Africa's highest peak, is a magnet for trekkers worldwide. Hike through diverse landscapes, from rainforest to volcanic scree, and conquer the "Roof of Africa" for a sunrise view that will forever etch itself in your memory. For a less strenuous climb, Mount Meru, a mini-Kilimanjaro offering stunning vistas and diverse ecosystems, promises an unforgettable adventure.

Tanzania's national parks and game reserves are more than just playgrounds for wildlife; they're portals to a wilder, more ancient world. So pack your sense of wonder, grab your binoculars, and prepare to be captivated by the unique wildlife, awe-inspiring water spots, and untamed spirit of this East African gem. Remember, the lions' roars will be your soundtrack, the endless plains on your canvas, and the thrill of discovery your guide as you explore the wild heart of Tanzania.

CHAPTER 5. Adventure and Outdoor Activities

Hiking and trekking opportunities

Tanzania, the jewel of East Africa, isn't just about spotting wildlife on thrilling safaris. It's a land begging to be explored on foot, where every step unveils a new vista, a hidden waterfall, or a glimpse into a world untouched by time. From scaling the continent's highest peak to weaving through misty rainforests, here's a taste of the incredible hiking and trekking opportunities Tanzania offers:

1. Conquer the Roof of Africa: Mount Kilimanjaro

It's the ultimate African challenge, the crown jewel of Tanzanian hikes: Mount Kilimanjaro. This snow-capped behemoth, piercing the clouds at 5,895 meters, beckons trekkers from around the world. Choose your route, from the scenic Marangu to the challenging Machame, and embark on a multi-day journey through diverse landscapes, from rainforest to volcanic scree. The summit reward? Breathtaking sunrises over endless plains and a sense of accomplishment that will stay with you forever.

2. Trek Through Untamed Eden: The Usambara Mountains

For those seeking a lush, off-the-beaten-path adventure, the Usambara Mountains whisper their secrets. This ancient range, draped in mist and draped in emerald forests, offers trails that wind past coffee plantations, hidden waterfalls, and traditional villages. Hike to the rim of the Shume Magozi Gorge, a natural amphitheater carved by time, or climb the highest peak, Mount Hanang, for panoramic views that stretch to the distant plains. Keep your eyes peeled for colobus monkeys swinging through the canopy and elephants lumbering through the undergrowth.

3. Explore the Volcanic Highlands: The Ngorongoro Crater and Beyond

The Ngorongoro Crater isn't just a wildlife haven; it's a hiker's paradise. Descend along the rim via the Lerai Forest trail, spotting buffaloes and elephants grazing below. Challenge yourself with the Crater Floor hike, a six-hour trek through diverse ecosystems, from grasslands to swamps. For a unique experience, climb the Ol Doinyo Lengai volcano, the only active volcano in Tanzania that erupts with molten lava – a true geological wonder.

4. Discover Hidden Waterfalls: The Mahale Mountains and Ruaha National Park

Imagine trekking through lush rainforests, the air thick with the scent of ferns and orchids, and then stumbling upon a hidden waterfall cascading into a turquoise pool. This is the magic of the Mahale Mountains, a remote gem bordering Lake Tanganyika. Hike through Kasakela Forest, spot chimpanzees swinging through the trees, and cool off under the refreshing spray of Mkombezi Falls. In Ruaha National Park, another hidden gem, trek along the Mwagusi River, discovering hidden waterfalls and swimming in natural pools that shimmer like emeralds.

5. Immerse Yourself in Culture: The Longido Highlands and Materuni Waterfalls

Hiking in Tanzania isn't just about conquering peaks and discovering waterfalls; it's about immersing yourself in the local culture. In the Longido Highlands, home to the Maasai people, hike alongside warriors on traditional cattle trails, learning about their way of life and ancient customs. Near Moshi, the gateway to Kilimanjaro, climb the Materuni Waterfalls, stopping to visit a traditional Chagga village along the way and savoring a local banana brew.

These are just a taste of the incredible hiking and trekking opportunities Tanzania offers. So lace up your boots, grab your backpack, and prepare to be awestruck by the raw beauty, diverse landscapes, and vibrant cultures that await you on the trails of this East African gem. Remember, it's not just about the destination; it's about the journey, the unexpected encounters, and the memories that will stay with you long after your boots are hung up.

Extra Tip: For the ultimate outdoor adventure, combine hiking with a wildlife safari. Many national parks offer multi-day treks that include game drives, allowing you to experience the best of both worlds.

Scuba diving and snorkeling in the Indian Ocean

Scuba Dreams and Snorkeling Bliss

Tanzania isn't just about savannas teeming with wildlife and snow-capped peaks piercing the skies. Beneath the turquoise embrace of the Indian Ocean lies a vibrant underwater world, an archipelago of coral reefs and marine marvels waiting to be discovered. Whether you're a seasoned scuba diver or a curious snorkeler dipping your toes in, Tanzania's coastline promises an aquatic adventure unlike any other.

1. Zanzibar: Spice Island's Dazzling Depths

Zanzibar, the spice-scented isle, isn't just about swaying palms and pristine beaches. Its coral reefs pulsate with life, home to technicolor fish darting through coral canyons and graceful turtles gliding through kelp forests. Dive into Mnemba Atoll, a protected marine reserve where vibrant coral gardens teem with fish life, or explore Nungwi's crystal-clear waters, spotting playful dolphins and curious sharks. For snorkelers, shallow reefs like Matemwe offer kaleidoscopic underwater worlds, perfect for a family splash.

2. Mafia Island: A Pristine Paradise Untouched

Mafia Island, a jewel nestled south of Zanzibar, whispers tales of hidden reefs and untouched beauty. Dive alongside whale sharks, the gentle giants of the ocean, in the Mafia Channel, or explore Kipumbwi Reef, a labyrinthine coral wonderland bursting with marine life. For snorkelers, Chole Bay beckons with its calm waters and colorful coral formations, where clownfish peek from anemones and seahorses sway with the tide.

3. Pemba Island: Manta Magic and Underwater Mysteries

Pemba Island, the less-traveled sister of Zanzibar, is a diver's haven. Manta rays, with majestic wings gliding through the blue, are regular visitors to Manta Point, while Nyerere Channel offers encounters with playful dolphins and schools of shimmering fish. Snorkelers can marvel at the coral gardens of Fundu Lagoon, a shallow underwater paradise buzzing with life, or explore Furahani Reef, a kaleidoscope of colors teeming with tropical fish.

4. Beyond the Reefs: Whaleshark Encounters and Shipwrecks

Tanzania's aquatic playground extends beyond coral reefs. Dive into the deep blue off Latham Island for a chance encounter with whale sharks, their immense forms gliding through the ocean like living submarines. History buffs can explore the German cruiser Königsberg, a sunken wreck off Mafia Island, or dive into the Kilwa Caves, a submerged city shrouded in ancient mysteries.

5. A Snorkeler's Serengeti: Beyond the Big Five

Snorkeling isn't just a prelude to diving; it's an adventure in its own right. Explore shallow reefs teeming with vibrant fish, spot playful turtles basking on the rocks, and marvel at the delicate beauty of coral formations. In Saadani National Park, you can even snorkel alongside elephants frolicking in the shallows – a truly once-in-a-lifetime experience.

So, whether you're a seasoned diver seeking adrenaline-pumping encounters or a curious snorkeler yearning for a glimpse into the underwater world, Tanzania's Indian Ocean promises an unforgettable aquatic adventure. Pack your fins, grab your mask, and prepare to be awestruck by the vibrant coral reefs, majestic creatures, and endless beauty that lie beneath the turquoise waves.

Bonus Tip: Remember, responsible diving and snorkeling are key to protecting Tanzania's underwater treasures. Choose eco-friendly operators, avoid touching marine life, and never take anything but memories from the reefs. Let's explore responsibly and ensure future generations can enjoy this aquatic paradise.

Canoeing and boating on Tanzania's lakes and rivers

Forget dusty trails and roaring engines – Tanzania holds a watery secret, a network of shimmering lakes and whispering rivers begging to be explored by canoe and boat. So ditch the jeep for a paddle or life vest and prepare to become part of the current, weave through reeds with hippos, watch elephants bathe in hidden pools, and witness the heartbeat of East Africa from the gentle sway of a canoe or the rhythmic hum of a boat engine.

1. Serengeti Symphony on the Mara River:

Imagine drifting down the Mara River, the legendary lifeline of the Serengeti, where hippos snort from the reeds and crocodiles bask on sun-drenched banks. This isn't just a boat ride; it's a front-row seat to nature's grandest opera. Witness the annual migration unfold before your eyes as wildebeests thunder across the horizon, hooves drumming a primal rhythm against the current.

2. Lake Manyara's Magical Maze:

Nestled in the Rift Valley's shadow, Lake Manyara unveils a serene paradise woven with tangled forests and glittering waters. Glide past playful monkeys chattering from the canopy, watch hippos wallow in shallows, and spot elegant tree-climbing lions surveying their domain from lofty branches. This watery labyrinth, teeming with birdlife and vibrant foliage, offers a unique perspective on Tanzanian wildlife.

3. Rufiji River: Unveiling Ruaha's Untamed Beauty:

Ruaha National Park, the forgotten giant of Tanzania, whispers its secrets from the banks of the mighty Rufiji River. Navigate meandering channels through tangled mangroves, home to elusive crocodiles and exotic birds, or witness elephants lumbering to the water's edge as the sun paints the sky gold. This boat safari promises an off-the-beaten-path adventure into the heart of Tanzania's wild.

4. Ngorongoro Crater: A Volcanic Jewel with Hidden Waters:

Descend into the Ngorongoro Crater, a volcanic Eden, and discover a different kind of watery haven. Paddle across the Magadi Lake, a soda lake shimmering like a mirage, surrounded by towering crater walls teeming with wildlife. Watch flamingoes dance on the edges, searching for algae in the salty waters, and be captivated by the unique ecosystem thriving within this volcanic gem.

5. Beyond the Big Five: Discovering Hidden Waterways:

Tanzania's watery adventures go beyond the iconic parks. Canoe through the papyrus swamps of Rubondo Island National Park, spotting chimpanzees swinging through trees and hippos emerging from the reeds. Navigate Lake Tanganyika, Africa's second-deepest lake, on a traditional dhow, encountering fishing villages and vibrant markets along the shores. Each river and lake whispers its tale, waiting to be discovered by adventurous paddlers and curious boaters.

So grab your paddles, settle into your boat, and prepare to be captivated by the tranquility and beauty of Tanzania's aquatic realm. From witnessing the migration from the river's edge to exploring hidden waterways teeming with life, these watery adventures offer a unique perspective on this East African gem. Remember, the gentle lapping of waves will be your soundtrack, the vastness of the water your canvas, and the thrill of discovery your guide as you navigate the liquid landscapes of Tanzania.

Bonus Tip: Be mindful of your impact on these fragile ecosystems. Choose eco-friendly operators, avoid disturbing wildlife, and leave only footprints as you paddle through paradise.

Hot air balloon safaris

Forget bumpy jeep rides and jostling crowds; Tanzania unveils its grandeur from a truly elevated perspective – aboard a hot air balloon. Imagine rising with the dawn, a gentle breeze lifting you above the savanna as the sun ignites the endless plains in a symphony of gold and crimson. This isn't just a safari; it's an ethereal dance with the sky, a silent serenade by nature's most breathtaking panoramas.

1. Soaring Above the Serengeti:

The Serengeti isn't just a park; it's a primordial pulse, and what better way to feel its rhythm than from a floating bubble overlooking the scene? Watch the Great Migration unfurl beneath you, millions of hooves drumming the earth as wildebeests and zebras chase life-giving rains. Spot predators stalking their prey across the golden grasslands, and witness the vastness of nature stretch beyond the horizon, untouched and untamed.

2. Ngorongoro's Volcanic Eden from Above:

Descend into the Ngorongoro Crater, a volcanic Eden, by hot air balloon. This isn't an entrance; it's a grand reveal. Float silently above the crater rim, witnessing the amphitheater below teeming with elephants, rhinos, and even the rare black rhino. Watch lions bask in the morning sun, buffalo herds graze on emerald grasslands, and feel the weight of millennia press down upon you from the ancient caldera walls.

3. Beyond the Big Five: Unveiling Hidden Treasures:

While the Serengeti and Ngorongoro hold the spotlight, Tanzania's aerial magic unfolds across hidden gems. Soar above Tarangire, where baobab trees stand like timeworn sentinels guarding herds of lumbering elephants. Float over Ruaha, the forgotten giant, where elusive leopards slink through the undergrowth and buffalo herds stretch across the plains like sun-dusted rivers. For a truly off-the-beaten-path adventure, ascend above Katavi, where crocodiles bask along the mighty Rukwa River, and a prehistoric tableau comes to life.

4. A Champagne Toast to Sunrise:

A balloon safari isn't just about the views; it's about the experience. Feel the gentle pull of the wind as you ascend, the coolness of the dawn airbrushing your cheeks. Sip on a glass of sparkling wine as the first rays of sunlight paint the sky with fiery hues. Share this aerial symphony with like-minded adventurers, a camaraderie forged in the shared wonder of seeing Tanzania from a celestial perch.

5. Memories That Take Flight:

Long after you touch down, the memories of your balloon safari will linger. The golden plains stretching endlessly beneath you, the sunbeams glinting off distant animals, the silence broken only by the whisper of the wind – these are moments that etch themselves onto your soul. So step into the basket, let go of the earth, and prepare to be captivated by the magic of Tanzania's hot air balloon safari – an experience that will redefine your travel adventures forever.

Bonus Tip: For the ultimate in exclusivity, consider a private balloon safari. Imagine drifting through the sky with your loved ones, a personal serenade by nature's grandest spectacle.

CHAPTER 6. Cultural Experiences

Tanzania's magic isn't confined to savannas teeming with wildlife or snow-capped peaks piercing the clouds. Beneath the vibrant surface lies a rich tapestry of cultural experiences, woven with ancient traditions, rhythmic music and dance, and captivating arts and crafts. So, pack your curiosity and wanderlust, and prepare to immerse yourself in the soul of Tanzania:

Unveiling the Soul of the Land: Encounters with Local Tribes

Tanzania isn't just a country; it's a mosaic of diverse tribes, each with its unique customs and languages. Witness the colorful Maasai warriors adorned in beaded jewelry, their rhythmic chants echoing across the plains. Learn about their nomadic way of life, their reverence for cattle, and their captivating jumping dances that defy gravity. In the remote villages of the Hadzabe and Datoga, step back in time to a hunter-gatherer lifestyle, where survival skills are honed and ancient traditions endure. Each encounter is a window into a different world, a chance to connect with the beating heart of Tanzania.

Traditional music and dance

When Rhythm Takes Over: The Power of Traditional Music and Dance

Tanzania's music isn't just background noise; it's a pulsating heartbeat, a vibrant tapestry of sounds that tell stories and stir emotions. Listen to the haunting melodies of the Maasai olindilai, a song flute that carries across the plains, or lose yourself in the infectious rhythms of the bongo drums, their beats echoing through vibrant village celebrations. Witness the graceful movements of the Sukuma ngoma dance, a mesmerizing display of strength and agility, or let the energy of the energetic Kuria ngoma wash over you, a celebration of life and community. Each beat, each step, is a testament to the cultural richness that defines Tanzania.

Arts and crafts

A Canvas of Creativity: Exploring Tanzania's Arts and Crafts

Tanzania's artistic spirit isn't confined to nature's beauty; it spills over into intricate beadwork, vibrant fabrics, and captivating sculptures. Wander through bustling markets like Mwenge in Dar es Salaam, where Maasai women weave intricate beaded jewelry, their fingers dancing with colorful threads. In Arusha, witness the transformative power of fire as skilled Makonde carvers bring ebony to life, creating masks and figurines that whisper ancient stories. Visit the bustling village of Tingatinga, where vibrant murals burst with life, each stroke a vibrant celebration of Tanzanian culture. Every souvenir isn't just a trinket; it's a piece of Tanzania's soul, a reminder of the creativity that flows through this East African gem.

Visiting Local Markets and Villages

Stepping into the Heartbeat: Visiting Local Markets and Villages

To truly understand a culture, you have to step into its heart. Explore bustling markets like Arusha Central Market, where the air is thick with the scent of spices and the chatter of vendors. Bargain for colorful fabrics, sample local delicacies like mandazi (fried dough), and lose yourself in the vibrant tapestry of daily life. Visit a traditional village like Mto Wa Mbu, where mud huts huddle together and children play in dusty streets. Share a meal with a local family, learn about their traditions, and witness the warmth and hospitality that defines Tanzanian culture. Each interaction is a bridge, a chance to connect with the human spirit that makes Tanzania so special.

So, go beyond the safaris and the sunsets. Dive into the soul of Tanzania, where tribes whisper their ancient stories, music pulsates with life, and art blossoms in every corner. Remember, the welcoming smiles will be your compass, the vibrant markets your canvas, and the shared stories your guide as you weave your cultural tapestry in the heart of Tanzania.

Extra Tip: Respect local customs and traditions. Dress modestly when visiting villages, ask permission before taking photographs, and embrace the spirit of cultural exchange with an open mind and a curious heart.

CHAPTER 7. Accommodation

Tanzania's accommodation scene isn't just about a place to rest your head – it's a chance to extend your safari experience, immersing yourself in diverse environments and unique atmospheres. Whether you crave luxurious pampering, a taste of safari life, or budget-friendly charm, Tanzania has a sleeping sanctuary waiting for you:

Luxurious Hotels and Resorts:

For those seeking five-star indulgence, Tanzania's coastal havens and vibrant cities offer havens of contemporary comfort. In Zanzibar, sip cocktails by infinity pools overlooking turquoise waters, indulge in rejuvenating spa treatments and savor gourmet cuisine in opulent settings. Dar es Salaam boasts sleek city hotels with rooftop bars and panoramic views, while Arusha provides a gateway to the wilderness with luxurious lodges offering personalized service and a touch of colonial elegance.

Safari Lodges and Tented Camps:

To truly feel the pulse of the wild, step into the world of safari lodges and tented camps. Imagine waking up to the trumpeting of elephants from your canvas cocoon in the Serengeti, or sipping sundowners overlooking the

Ngorongoro Crater from your private balcony in a traditional lodge. Each camp and lodge is a thoughtfully designed haven, blending comfort with authenticity. Choose from rustic elegance with crackling fireplaces and starlit dinners, to eco-friendly camps designed to minimize their footprint on the landscape.

Guesthouses and Budget Options:

Tanzania's charm extends beyond luxury, offering welcoming guesthouses and budget-friendly options for off-the-beaten-path adventurers and solo travelers. In bustling markets like Kariakoo, find hidden gems tucked away down alleyways, offering clean rooms and local flavor at affordable prices. Explore historic towns like Stone Town in Zanzibar, where charming guesthouses housed in centuries-old buildings boast character and a vibrant cultural touch. For nature lovers, eco-friendly lodges and campsites offer basic but comfortable accommodations amidst stunning landscapes.

Extra Tip: Consider your priorities when choosing accommodation. If wildlife viewing is your top priority, prioritize location within parks or reserves. For those seeking relaxation, coastal resorts or lodges nestled amidst rolling hills provide a serene escape. Remember, your accommodation choice is a chance to personalize your Tanzanian adventure.

From beachfront bungalows to star-gazing tented camps, Tanzania's accommodation landscape is as diverse as its landscapes. So, whether you crave opulent indulgence, rustic charm, or budget-friendly adventures, this East African gem has a perfect hideaway waiting to embrace you.

CHAPTER 8. Dining and Cuisine

Tanzania's culinary scene is as vibrant and diverse as its landscapes. It's not just about fueling your safari adventures; it's about a captivating dance with spices, an exploration of ancient traditions, and a chance to savor the soul of this East African gem. So, prepare your taste buds and open your horizons:

Traditional Tanzanian dishes

Unveiling the Heart of Tanzania: Traditional Tanzanian Dishes

Dive into the heart of Tanzanian cuisine with its star player – ugali, the cornmeal porridge that serves as the base for many meals. Savor it alongside nyama choma, grilled meat bursting with smoky flavors, or pair it with mchuzi, a flavorful stew featuring vegetables, groundnuts, and spices. Sample ndizi-nyama, a sweet and savory dish of plantains simmered with meat, or try pilau, the aromatic rice pilaf with its Persian influences. Each bite is a testament to Tanzania's cultural tapestry, a melody of flavors that tells stories of tradition and community.

Local Restaurants and Street Food

Where the Locals Feast: Popular Local Restaurants and Street Food

Skip the generic buffets and dive into the soul of Tanzania through its local food scene. Explore bustling markets like Kariakoo in Dar es Salaam, where aroma-laden stalls tempt with sizzling samosas, crispy mandazi (fried dough), and flavorful chapati, the flatbread that can be enjoyed plain or filled with savory delights. Venture into Stone Town in Zanzibar, where fragrant spice shops tempt with their exotic scents and local eateries dish up seafood curries and coconut-infused delicacies. Don't be afraid to try street food like grilled corn on the cob (mkate wa mahindi) or skewered meat (mishikaki), seasoned with just the right touch of chili for a fiery kick.

Dietary Considerations and Food Safety Tips

Catering to Every Palate: Dietary Considerations and Food Safety Tips

Tanzania welcomes diverse appetites, and dietary considerations are taken seriously. Vegetarians and vegans rejoice with lentil stews, fresh salads, and vegetable-packed samosas. Travelers with allergies or other dietary restrictions can find options in most restaurants, and gluten-free choices are becoming increasingly available. When it comes to food safety, stick to reputable vendors and cooked dishes, especially during street food adventures. Carry bottled water and choose fruits you can peel yourself. Remember, a little local advice goes a long way – don't hesitate to ask vendors or restaurant staff for their recommendations.

Bonus Tip: Embrace the spirit of sharing. Traditional Tanzanian meals are often communal affairs, served on large platters to be enjoyed together. Don't be afraid to dig in with your hands, it's the perfect way to connect with locals and experience the warmth of Tanzania's culinary culture.

From starlit dinners under the Serengeti sky to bustling market feasts, Tanzania's culinary scene is an adventure waiting to be savored. So, open your mind, tickle your taste buds, and embark on a delicious journey through the heart of this vibrant East African gem.

CHAPTER 9. Shopping and Souvenirs

Tanzania's treasures aren't just confined to its wildlife and landscapes; its markets and craft stalls brim with unique souvenirs and handcrafted wonders begging to be discovered. So, ditch the generic keychains and pack your wanderlust – a shopping adventure awaits you in this East African gem:

Unique Tanzanian products and handicrafts

Beyond the Bling: Unveiling Unique Tanzanian Products and Handicrafts

Tanzania's artistic spirit takes form in vibrant fabrics, intricate beadwork, and captivating sculptures. In bustling markets like Kariakoo in Dar es Salaam, lose yourself in a kaleidoscope of colors. Admire the Maasai women weaving beaded jewelry, watch Makonde carvers breathe life into ebony masks, and be mesmerized by the vibrant hues of Tingatinga paintings. Explore Zanzibar's spice shops, where the air is thick with exotic aromas, and pick up unique blends to recreate the island's culinary magic back home. For the truly unique, seek out Makonde ebony combs, hand-forged knives from

Dodoma, or hand-woven baskets from Babati – each piece is a whisper of Tanzania's cultural heritage.

Best Places to Shop for Souvenirs

b. Finding Your Treasure Trove: Best Places to Shop for Souvenirs

Step beyond the generic tourist shops and discover the soul of Tanzania through its authentic markets and village cooperatives. In Arusha, the Maasai Market pulsates with vibrant life, while Mto Wa Mbu village offers a glimpse into traditional crafts like pottery and basket weaving. Zanzibar's Stone Town whispers ancient stories within its labyrinthine streets, where spice shops and artisan workshops invite exploration. Don't be afraid to venture off the beaten path – remote villages often reveal hidden gems known only to locals. Remember, the most authentic souvenirs are often found away from the crowds, waiting to be unearthed by adventurous souls.

Bargaining Tips

c. Mastering the Art of the Bargain: Bargaining Tips

Tanzanian markets are a symphony of colors, scents, and chatter, and bargaining is simply part of the dance. Embrace the spirit of friendly banter and approach negotiations with a smile. Start with a fair offer, lower your price steadily, and be prepared to walk away if the deal isn't right. Remember, respect goes a long way – a friendly demeanor and polite communication will often secure the best price. And don't forget to celebrate even small victories – after all, bargaining is as much about the experience as it is about the price.

Extra Tip: When choosing souvenirs, prioritize sustainability. Opt for eco-friendly crafts made from recycled materials or natural fibers. Support local artisans by buying directly from them, ensuring the profits stay within the community

CHAPTER 10 Health and Safety

Tips for a Worry-Free Tanzanian Adventure

Tanzania is a generally safe country for responsible travelers, but a few precautions ensure a smooth and healthy adventure:

- Pack essentials: Bring insect repellent, sunscreen, a first-aid kit, and any necessary medications.
- Drink bottled water: Avoid tap water unless proven safe.
- Be sun-smart: Cover up during peak sun hours and stay hydrated.
- Respect local customs: Dress modestly, especially in villages.
- Keep valuables safe: Don't flash cash or expensive jewelry.
- Follow park regulations: Stick to designated paths and respect wildlife viewing guidelines.
- Choose reputable operators: Ensure tour companies and accommodations are licensed and follow ethical practices.

By staying informed and making responsible choices, you can ensure a safe and fulfilling Tanzanian adventure, filled with unforgettable memories and treasures that will bring back the magic of this East African gem long after you return home.

Embarking on a Tanzanian adventure promises breathtaking landscapes, thrilling wildlife encounters, and cultural immersion. But before you pack your bags and book your flights, ensuring your health and safety is essential. Here's what you need to know:

Vaccination Requirements and Medical Facilities:

Consult your doctor or a travel clinic well in advance to determine necessary vaccinations. Yellow fever and rabies are mandatory for most travelers, and hepatitis A and B, typhoid, and meningococcal meningitis are recommended depending on your itinerary and health background.

Tanzania boasts modern medical facilities in major cities, but access to care can be limited in remote areas. Consider travel insurance and pack any prescription medications you need. Remember, it's wise to bring basic over-the-counter medications for common ailments like diarrhea and mosquito bites.

Malaria Prevention and Other Health Considerations:

Malaria is prevalent in parts of Tanzania, especially during the rainy season. Consult your doctor for the recommended anti-malarial medication and implement preventive measures like using mosquito nets, wearing long sleeves and pants at dusk and dawn, and applying insect repellent with DEET.

Other health considerations include staying hydrated, avoiding direct sunlight during peak hours, and being mindful of food and water hygiene. Stick to bottled water, eat cooked food, and be wary of street vendors if unsure about their practices.

Emergency Contacts and Local Laws:

Before you depart, save the emergency contact numbers for your embassy, local police, and any medical facilities you might need. Familiarize yourself with Tanzanian laws and customs. Dress modestly, especially in religious sites and villages. Avoid taking drugs, as penalties can be severe.

Respect wildlife viewing regulations and understand the risks of approaching wild animals, even harmless-looking ones. Most importantly, trust your gut and stay alert, avoiding risky situations.

CHAPTER 11. Language and Culture

Bridging the Gap in Tanzania

Embracing the local language and cultural nuances enriches your Tanzanian experience. Here are some insights:

Language

Swahili is the national language, and while English is spoken in tourist areas, learning basic Swahili phrases goes a long way. Greet people with "Jambo," thank them with "Asante," and learn numbers for bargaining. Be patient and don't hesitate to use hand gestures and smiles – communication transcends language barriers.

Cultural Etiquette

Respect is paramount in Tanzanian culture. Dress modestly, covering shoulders and knees. Greet elders first, avoid pointing, and refrain from public displays of affection. Learn about local customs and traditions, and embrace the opportunity to observe and participate in cultural events.

Cultural Sensitivity

Be mindful of local beliefs and traditions. Ask permission before taking photographs, particularly of people and sacred sites. Haggling is expected in markets but do so politely and respectfully. Remember, you're a guest in their land, so treat it with respect and a spirit of cultural exchange.

By prioritizing health and safety, embracing the local language, and respecting cultural norms, you pave the way for a safe, fulfilling, and enriching Tanzanian adventure. Remember, a little preparation goes a long way, and the warm Tanzanian hospitality will embrace you as you navigate this captivating East African gem.

Conclusion

As the sun dips below the Serengeti plains, painting the sky in fiery hues, it's time to reflect on the magic that is Tanzania. This East African gem isn't just a collection of landscapes and wildlife; it's a symphony of experiences, a vibrant tapestry woven with ancient traditions, rhythmic music, and breathtaking beauty.

From the thunderous hooves of the Great Migration to the whispered secrets of hidden villages, Tanzania has captured your heart, ignited your adventurous spirit, and awakened your senses to a world beyond the ordinary. You've danced with the Maasai, tasted the spice-kissed flavors of local cuisine, and marveled at the celestial ballet of hot air balloons against the rising sun.

This journey wasn't just about checking off destinations; it was about feeling the pulse of the wild, connecting with a vibrant culture, and creating memories that will forever shimmer in your soul. As you pack your bags, filled with souvenirs and stories, remember that Tanzania isn't just a place you visited; it's a place that has seeped into your being, leaving an indelible mark on your spirit.

So carry the warmth of Tanzanian hospitality, the awe of its untouched landscapes, and the rhythm of its vibrant culture with you wherever you go. Share your stories, inspire others to embark on their Tanzanian adventures, and remember that this isn't goodbye, but rather a "tutaonana"—a see you soon—to the land that stole your heart and whispered its secrets in the wind.

Tanzania, with its endless skies and open arms, welcomes you back, promising new adventures and unforgettable experiences. Until then, let the memories continue to dance in your mind, reminding you that the magic of this East African gem lives on, not just in photographs and souvenirs, but in the echo of laughter, the thrill of discovery, and the warmth of a land that forever holds a piece of your soul.

Printed in Great Britain
by Amazon